D1394722

Making Science Work

Finding Out About Energy

Terry Jennings

Illustrations by
Peter Smith and
Catherine Ward

LONDON BOROUGH OF BARKING AND DAGENHAM
SCHOOL LIBRARIES

Belitha Press

First published in the United Kingdom in 1996 by
Belitha Press Ltd, London House, Great Eastern Wharf,
Parkgate Road, London SW11 4NQ
First published 1996 by Cynthia Parzych Publishing Inc, New York
Copyright © 1996 Cynthia Parzych Publishing Inc

Text copyright © 1996 Terry Jennings

All rights reserved. No part of this book may be reproduced or utilized in any form or
by any means, electronic or mechanical, including photocopying, recording, or by any
information storage and retrieval system without permission in writing from the publisher,
except by a reviewer who may quote brief passages in a review.

Designed by Arcadia Consultants.

Printed and bound in Spain.

British Library Cataloguing in Publication Data for this book
is available from the British Library.

ISBN 1 85561 530 4

LONDON BOROUGH OF BARKING
AND DAGENHAM
SCHOOL LIBRARIES

No. | PL 531601
Class | 531

Words in **bold** appear in the glossary on page 31.

PHOTO CREDITS
Art Directors Photo Library: 4 bottom (© Ron Watts),
5 top, 7, 21 left (© Craig Ames), 21 right, 24 (© Brian
Vikander)
B & U International Picture Service: 5 bottom, 24
The Environmental Picture Library: 8 top (C Westwood
photo), 8 bottom (Martin Bond photo), 28 (Robert Brook
photo), 29 (M Bond photo)
General Motors Corporation: 20
Jennings, Dr Terry: 4 top, 14
Peter Arnold, Inc: 11 (© Kevin Schafer)
Usine Maremotrice de la Rance, photo by
Michel Bregaud, © La Phototheque EDF: 19

Warning:
It is safe to experiment with torch batteries
(but not rechargeable ones).
Never play with other electricity sources.
They could kill you.

Contents

Energy everywhere

We use **energy** every day. We use energy when we walk or run. We even use energy when we are asleep. We use this energy to keep us warm. Energy lets us breathe. It keeps our heart working. The energy our body needs comes from food. We use energy to cook. We use energy to run cars and trucks, to grow food and to build homes.

Chemical energy changing to movement energy in a tractor.

Using energy to run computers

There are many different kinds of energy. Heat and light are kinds of energy. So are sound, electricity, movement and chemical energy. We cannot make energy. We can only turn one kind of energy into another.

Chemical energy from petrol changing to movement energy in cars.

Using energy to play

Much of the energy we use comes from coal, oil or gas. These are called **fossil fuels**. Coal was formed millions of years ago when thick forests grew in marshy ground. When the trees and other plants died, they sank into the mud. They were pushed deep under the ground and slowly turned into coal. Coal has a lot of chemical energy. It burns slowly with great heat.

Inside a coal mine

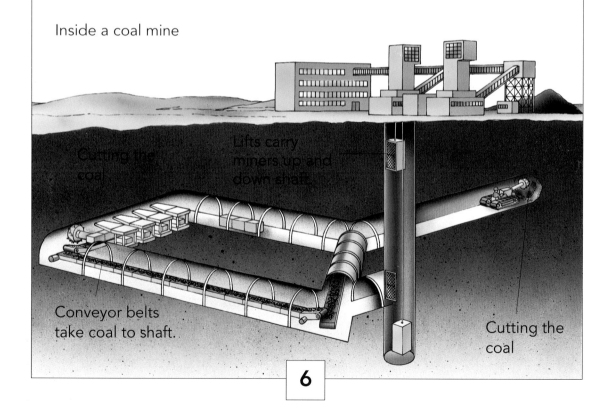

Cutting the coal

Lifts carry miners up and down shaft.

Conveyor belts take coal to shaft.

Cutting the coal

Oil and **natural gas** were made from the bodies of tiny sea creatures that died millions of years ago. They sank to the bottom of the ocean and slowly turned into oil or gas. Oil and natural gas have a lot of energy. They burn and give off a lot of heat. We are using up fossil fuels fast. One day none of them will be left.

An oil rig

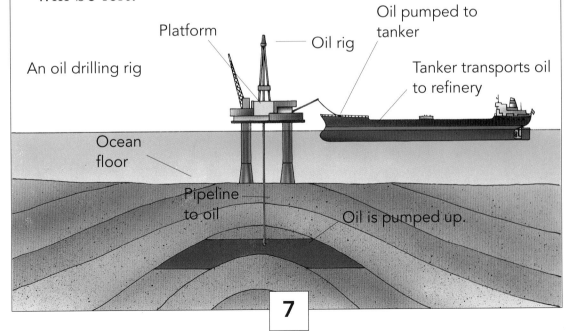

An oil drilling rig

Platform

Oil rig

Oil pumped to tanker

Tanker transports oil to refinery

Ocean floor

Pipeline to oil

Oil is pumped up.

When we burn fossil fuels, we dirty or pollute, the air with gases. These gases are given off when fossil fuels are burned. The gases are harmful to people. At the same time, the rain is made **acid**. The acid rain damages trees, lakes and buildings.

A building damaged by acid rain

Factories and power stations produce gases.

Making electricity causes **pollution**. This is because most electricity is made by burning fossil fuels. Some gases from fossil fuels may be making the Earth hotter. If the Earth becomes too hot, the **climate** will change.

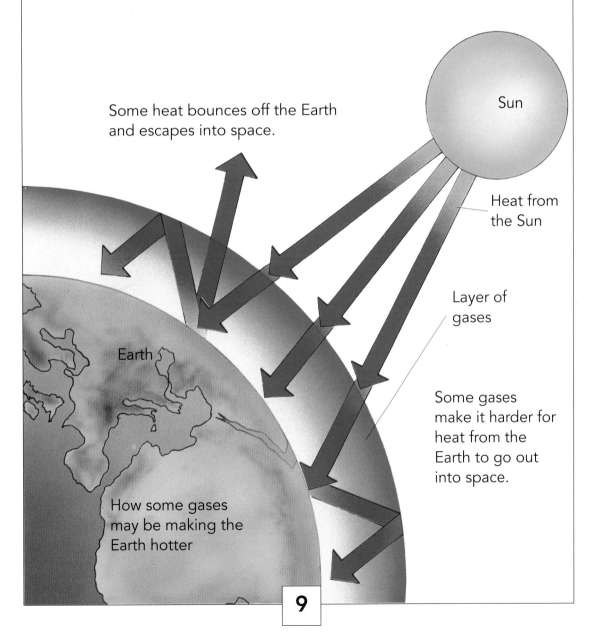

Some heat bounces off the Earth and escapes into space.

Sun

Heat from the Sun

Layer of gases

Earth

Some gases make it harder for heat from the Earth to go out into space.

How some gases may be making the Earth hotter

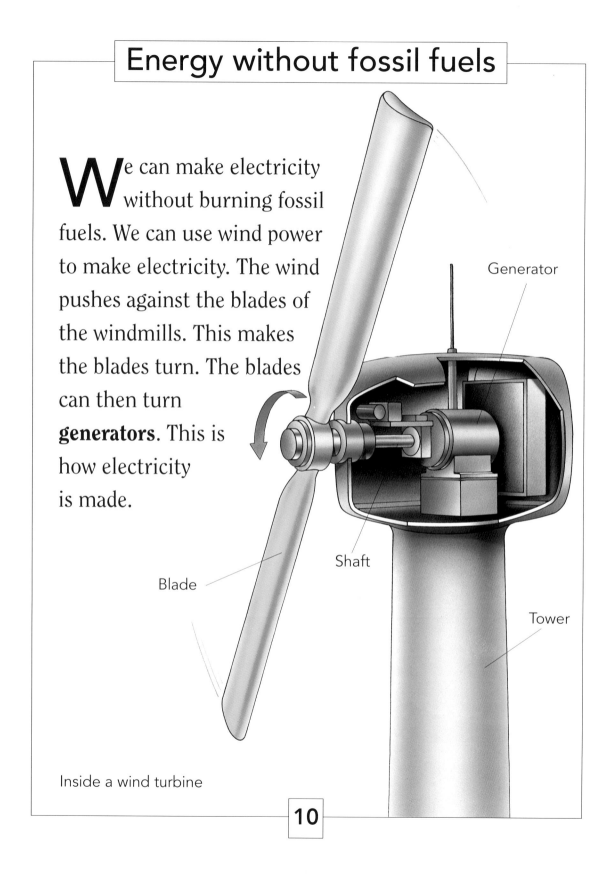

Energy without fossil fuels

We can make electricity without burning fossil fuels. We can use wind power to make electricity. The wind pushes against the blades of the windmills. This makes the blades turn. The blades can then turn **generators**. This is how electricity is made.

Generator

Shaft

Blade

Tower

Inside a wind turbine

Windmills are cheap to run. The energy of the wind is free. This kind of energy will never run out. It does not cause air pollution. But the wind alone cannot provide us with all the energy the world needs.

One windmill cannot make much electricity. We need many large windmills or wind **turbines** to make enough electricity for a small town.

These wind turbines make electricity.

Make a windmill

What to do

1 Cut out a square of paper.

2 Draw a line across the square from corner to corner. Draw another line between the other corners.

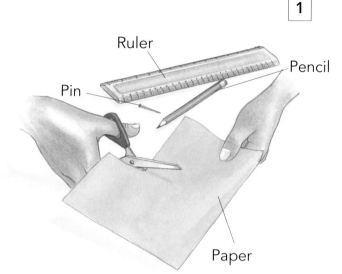

Ruler

Pencil

Pin

Paper

3 Make a pinhole beside the line in each corner.

4 Cut halfway down each line.

5 Fold the four points with pinholes into the centre.

6 Push the pin through the holes and the centre of the square. Then push it into the rubber on the end of a pencil. Blow on the windmill. The blades will spin. Try the windmill outside on a windy day. Make large and small windmills. Which spins faster?

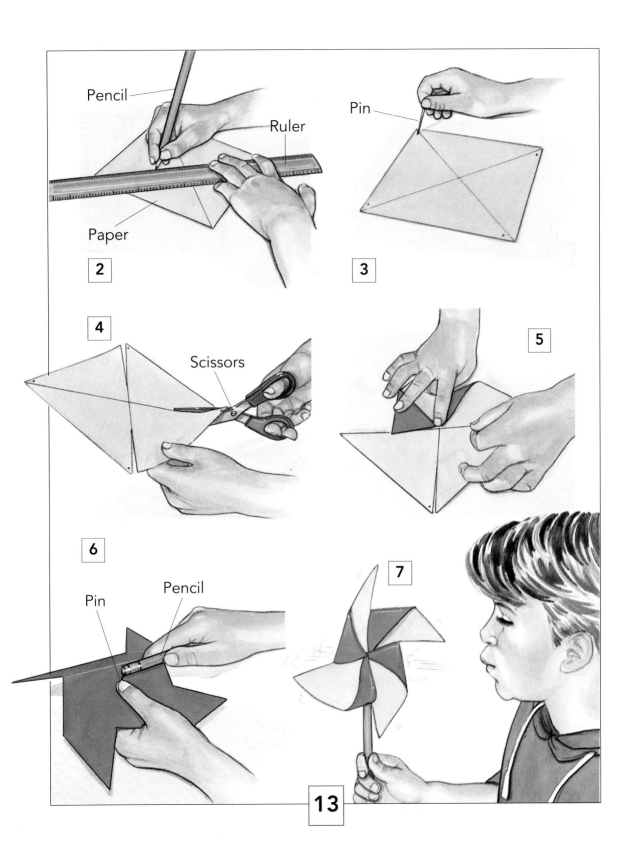

Pencil

Ruler

Paper

2

Pin

3

4

Scissors

5

6

Pin

Pencil

7

13

When rain falls on mountains, it makes rushing rivers. A rushing river has a lot of movement energy.

Some power stations use energy from moving water. They are called **hydroelectric power stations**. Usually a **dam** is built across a river valley. The water goes into a large lake or **reservoir**. When electricity is needed, gates are opened. The water rushes through tunnels in the dam. The water turns turbines. The turbines turn generators which change movement energy into electrical energy.

A hydroelectric power station

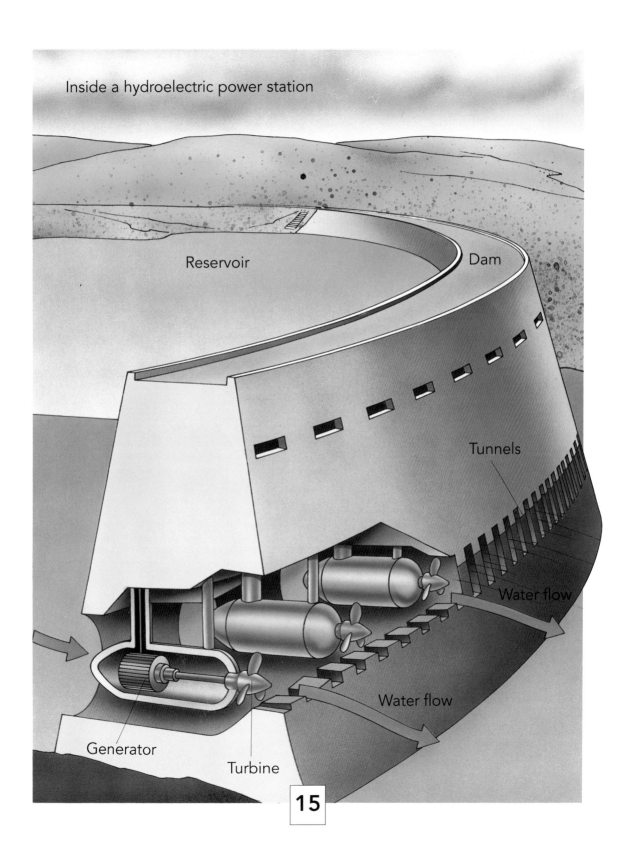

Inside a hydroelectric power station

Reservoir

Dam

Tunnels

Water flow

Water flow

Generator

Turbine

15

Make a water turbine

What to do

1 Ask an adult to cut the bottom off a large plastic bottle. Cut the bottom of the bottle to make four blades.

2 Make two holes halfway down the bottle.

3 Ask an adult to make holes through two corks with a nail.

4 Now ask them to cut four slits in one of the corks.

5 Push the blades into the slits.

6 Lay your turbine inside the bottle. Carefully push a knitting needle into one of the holes in the bottle. Then push it through the cork and out of the other hole. The second cork will keep your turbine in place.

7 Run a small stream of water on to the blades. Watch what happens.

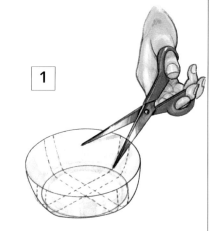

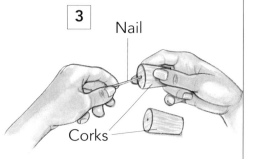

Plastic bottle

Hole

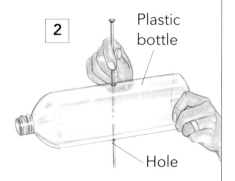

Nail

Corks

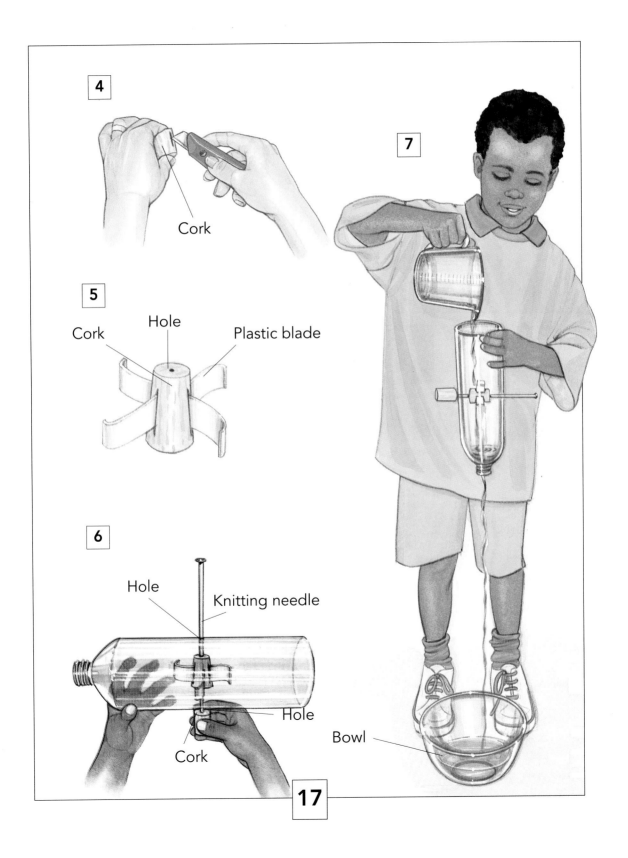

4

Cork

5

Cork   Hole   Plastic blade

6

Hole   Knitting needle

Hole

Cork

7

Bowl

17

The oceans can be used to make electricity. Waves can be very powerful. Waves form when the wind blows over the water's surface. Wave energy can be made to move a wave machine. The wave machine turns generators which change movement energy into electrical energy.

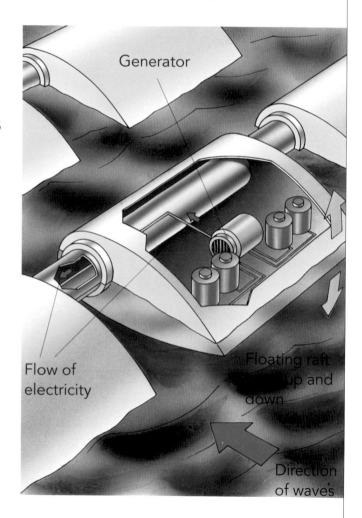

Generator

Flow of electricity

Floating raft up and down

Direction of waves

Inside a wave machine

At the seaside there are **tides**. Tides make the water move up and down the shore. The energy of the tides can be used. A barrier is built across a river where it reaches the ocean. The pushes and pulls of the tide turn turbines.

A tidal **power station** in France

The turbines turn generators which change movement energy into electrical energy.

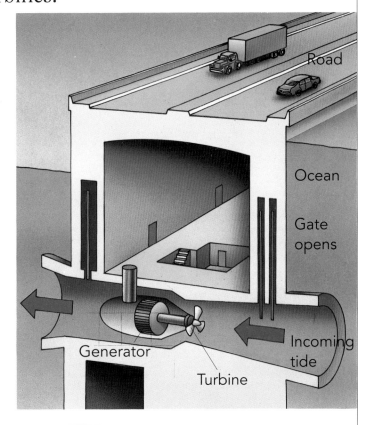

Road

Ocean

Gate opens

Incoming tide

Generator

Turbine

Inside a tidal power station

The Sun gives off a lot of energy. We can use energy from the Sun. We call it **solar power**. Your calculator, watch or radio may run on a **solar cell**. A solar cell uses light from the Sun. It changes the light energy into electricity.

A car can be powered by solar cells. Solar cells make electricity that is used to drive the car.

This car is solar-powered.

A power station can have thousands of solar cells. The solar cells each make a little electricity. Thousands of solar cells can make enough electricity for a small town.

Solar panels trap some of the Sun's energy. They warm the water that passes through the panels. These panels make hot water without fuel when the Sun shines.

A solar power station that uses solar cells.

Solar panels

Using solar panels

What to do

1 Take four foil trays. You need two large ones and two small ones. Paint the inside of one large tray and one small tray. Let them dry.

2 Set the four trays in the sun.

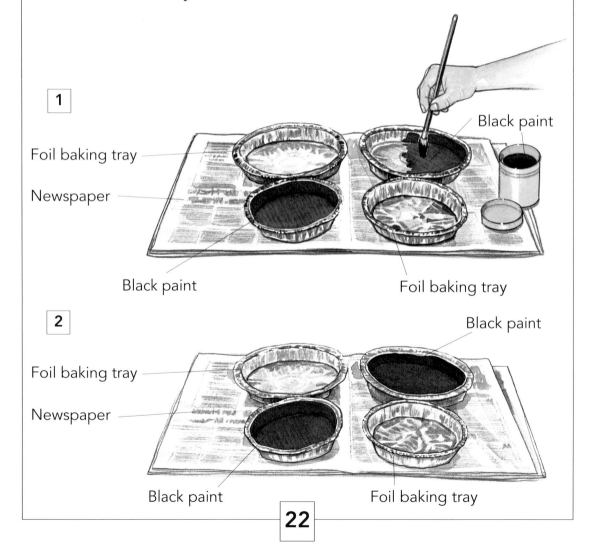

1

Foil baking tray

Newspaper

Black paint

Black paint

Foil baking tray

2

Foil baking tray

Newspaper

Black paint

Black paint

Foil baking tray

3

water

4

Thermometer

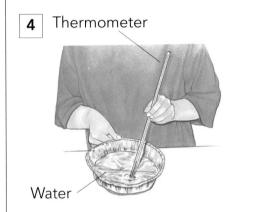

Water

3 Pour 100 ml of water into each tray.

4 Use a thermometer to measure the temperature of the water in each tray.

5 Cover the trays with plastic wrap. Leave them for about an hour.

6 Remove the plastic wrap. Lift the tray so the water runs into a corner. Use a thermometer to measure the temperature in each tray. Which tray was best at catching the Sun's energy?

5

Plastic wrap

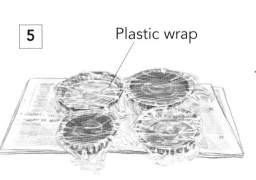

6

Thermometer

Plastic wrap

Geothermal power

The rocks deep inside the Earth are hot. The water that passes over these rocks is hot too. We can use this hot water on the Earth's surface. Some countries have natural hot springs or **geysers** that push hot water and steam to the Earth's surface.

Scientists have laid down pipes to hot rocks. They pump cold water down one pipe. The hot rocks heat the water. The hot water is then pumped back up. It is used to heat houses and to make electricity. This kind of power is called **geothermal power**.

A geyser

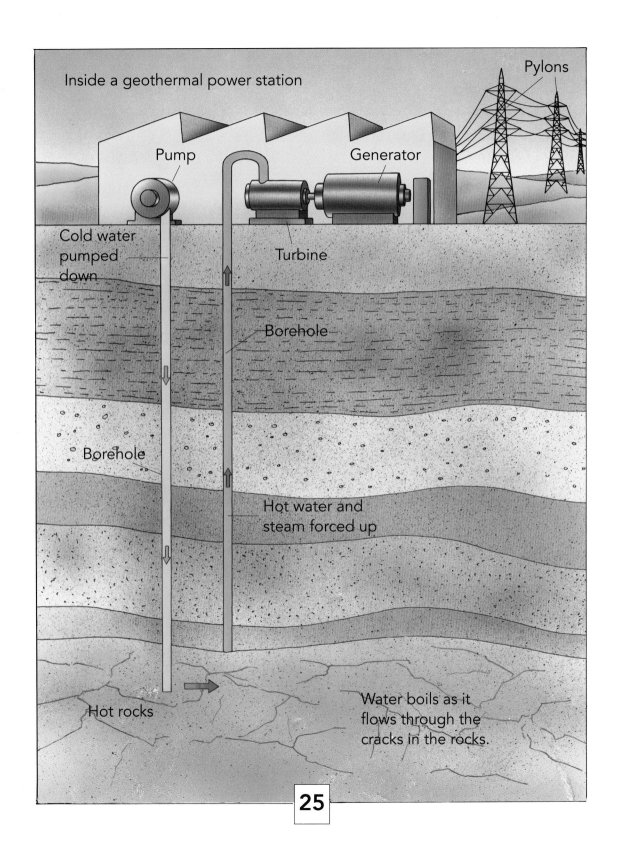

Inside a geothermal power station

Pylons

Pump

Generator

Cold water pumped down

Turbine

Borehole

Borehole

Hot water and steam forced up

Hot rocks

Water boils as it flows through the cracks in the rocks.

Heating pebbles

What to do

1 Put some clean pebbles in a metal baking tray.
Ask an adult to place the tray on a hot plate or in the
oven. Leave the tray of pebbles for about five minutes.

1 Clean pebbles

Baking tray

2 Half fill a metal bowl
with cold water. Measure
the temperature.

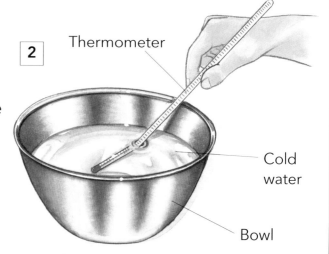

2 Thermometer

Cold
water

Bowl

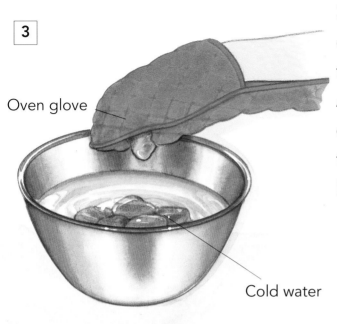

Oven glove

Cold water

3 Ask an adult to use oven gloves to pick up the hot tray of pebbles. An adult must help you drop the pebbles into the cold water one by one.

4 Measure the temperature again. Is the water hotter or colder? Feel the pebbles. What happened to their heat energy?

Thermometer

Energy from rubbish

Most rubbish is put into holes in the ground.

Rubbish can be used to make energy. Most rubbish is put into huge holes in the ground. It is then buried. As the rubbish rots, it gives off a gas. This gas is called **methane**. Methane can be burned and used to heat water. The hot water can be used to heat houses.

Rubbish can also be burned to make heat. It is burned in special furnaces. The heat can boil water to make steam. The steam moves turbines and generators. Turbines and generators make electricity. This is a good way to save fossil fuels. It is also a good way to get rid of rubbish. But there is a problem. Burning rubbish gives off gases. These gases pollute the air.

This power station burns rubbish to make electricity.

Saving energy

What to do

1 Turn off lights when they are not needed.

2 Carefully sort your rubbish. Take old paper, glass and metal to be recycled.

3 If you feel cold, put on extra clothing.

4 Ride a bicycle or walk short distances rather than go by car. This will save energy and help keep you fit.

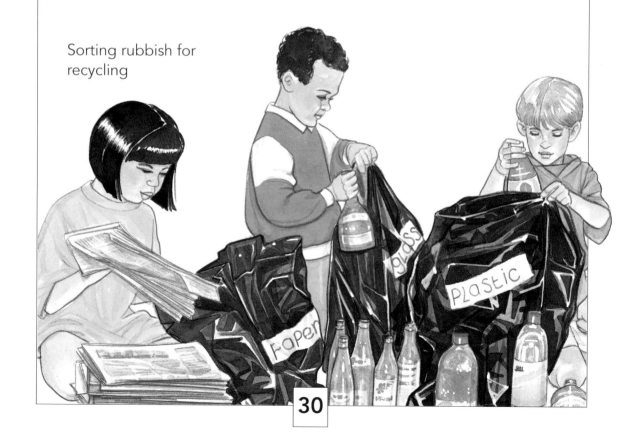

Sorting rubbish for recycling

Glossary

Acid A kind of chemical.

Carbon dioxide One of the gases in the air. Carbon dioxide is made when living things breathe and when fuels burn.

Climate The kind of weather that a place has throughout the year.

Dam A wall built across a river. It holds back the water and makes a reservoir.

Energy The ability something has to do work. There are many different forms of energy. Energy can be changed from one form to another.

Fossil fuel A fuel such as coal, oil or natural gas. It formed from the remains of living things millions of years old.

Fuel Anything that is burned to make heat energy such as coal, oil, gas or wood.

Generator A machine for changing movement energy into electrical energy.

Geothermal power Energy that comes from the heat deep inside the Earth.

Geyser Hot water that shoots out of the ground.

Hydroelectric power station A power station that makes electricity from the energy of moving water.

Methane A gas that has no smell or colour. It is used as a fuel.

Natural gas A gas found underground. It is a fossil fuel that contains a lot of methane.

Oil A liquid found underground. Oil is a fossil fuel. It is also used to make machinery run more smoothly. Petrol comes from oil.

Pollution Anything that makes the air, water, or the soil dirty.

Power station A large building where electricity is made.

Reservoir A large lake in which water for drinking, making electricity, or watering crops is stored.

Solar cell A device that changes sunlight into electrical energy.

Solar panel A device that absorbs energy from the Sun and uses it to heat water.

Solar power Energy from the heat or light of the Sun.

Tides The rise and fall of the level of the oceans.

Turbine A machine that is turned by air, gas, water or steam.

Index